# SUPER COOPE
# THE STANLEY CUP

written by Jack Gates

illustrated by Daniela Frongia

Ashland Ink

Published by Ashland Ink Publishing
209 West 2nd Street #177
Fort Worth TX 76102
www.ashlandink.com

Published in the United States of America

ISBN: 978-1-963514-07-0 (paperback)
ISBN: 978-1-963514-08-7 (hardback)

To Cooper,

Thank you for being a great friend and making the world a better place. I know you're going to continue to inspire everyone around you. Keep being super!

From,
Jack

Cooper was a fun, happy boy who was full of life. He loved being with his friends playing at the park, but he was most excited when they all gathered in front of the television to watch his favorite sport, hockey. One evening, they all jumped on the couch as Cooper screamed,

"WHO'S READY FOR SOME HOCKEY?"

Now some people might think that Cooper is different than other kids. When he was only two years old, the doctors told him that he had a disease called MPS 4A.

Feeling scared, Cooper asked what that meant.

"Your bones don't grow the same way as other kids, but don't let that stop you from dreaming big!"

"I'M JUST LIKE YOU," says Cooper when someone asks.

Later, as Cooper watched the Colorado Avalanche game on television, his eyes began to sparkle with hope. Leaning in close to the television, Cooper whispered,

"ONE DAY, I'LL BE OUT THERE."

Imagining the crowd cheering for him, Cooper began to dash through the living room shooting a sock into a makeshift net. Then he shouted,

"HE SHOOTS!"

"HE SCORES!"

At tryouts the next week, Cooper had to sit in the stands and watch his friends tryout. Because of his condition, he could not play. Cooper sighed,

"MOM, I WISH I COULD JOIN THEM."

Not long after that, Cooper needed to have surgery to help him feel better. He was not allowed to leave his bed in the hospital for a very long time.

"I'm so bored and I want to play with my friends. It's tough not moving around much," Cooper said. He was lonely and missed the days when he could run and play without worry.

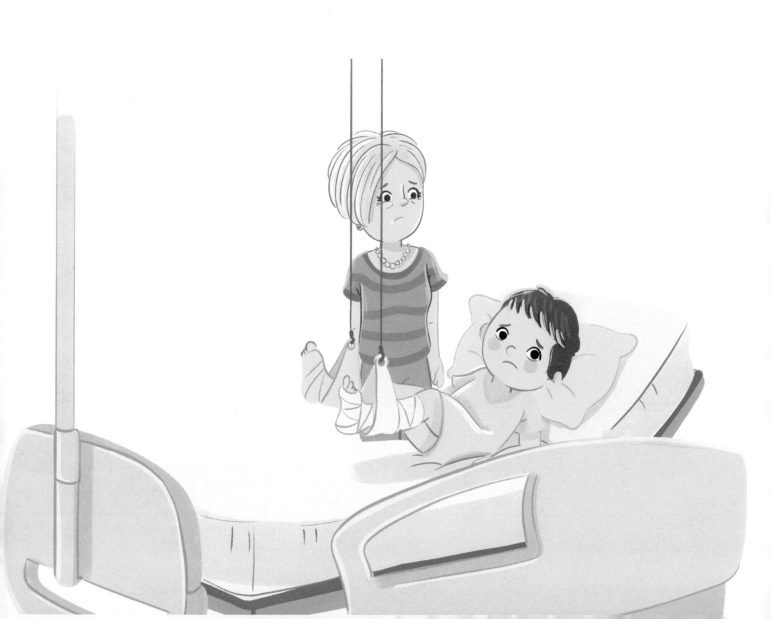

One day, Cooper received an incredible surprise visitor, Cale Makar from the Colorado Avalanche! A huge smile immediately appeared on Cooper's face.

"Never give up, Cooper. We're all cheering for you," Cale said, encouraging Cooper as he handed him a signed Jersey.

With a new nickname, **SUPER COOPER** , he finally got to go home where he quickly went back to practicing.

"WATCH ME GO, MOM!"

said Cooper as his mom recorded his every move.

Upon meeting his service dog, Velocity, Cooper said, "Every superhero needs a sidekick, right Velocity?"

The two quickly became an unstoppable duo and immediate best friends.

With Velocity by his side, Cooper continued to practice.

He practiced all day...

... and all night.

During his weekly hospital visits, Cooper's friends came by after school. They turned the hallway into their own private hockey rink. Even his mom and the nurses wanted to play!

# "THANK YOU FOR BEING SUCH GOOD FRIENDS,"

Cooper said with a smile so bright, it shined brighter than the braces he was wearing on his neck and back.

One day, his mom came into his room with some exciting news. "Guess what, Cooper? The hospital is granting you one wish because you were so brave. We get to go watch the Avalanche play in the Stanley Cup Finals!"

Overjoyed, Cooper could hardly believe he was going to get to see his favorite team play in person!

# "THIS IS A DREAM COME TRUE!"

At the game, Cooper pressed against the glass, wide-eyed, and marveling. "I can't believe I'm actually here watching my heroes!"

When Cale Makar was injured late in the game, tensions rose. The team frantically looked for someone to fill his skates.

Wincing in pain, Cale spotted Cooper in the stands. He tapped his coach and said, "Let Super Cooper play. I've seen what he can do. He's our guy."

As he dressed in his gear, Cooper thought of all the challenges he had overcome at the hospital. "Are you ready," he heard as the coach walked into the locker room.

"I've been through tougher battles," thought Cooper, "I can do this."

Facing the ice, Cooper remembered Cale's words.
"You got this, Cooper. Just believe in yourself."

Suddenly the crowd began to chant,

"SUPER COOPER!"

Stepping onto the ice, he felt a rush of excitement and nerves.

With the game hanging in the balance, Cooper focused.

"THIS IS MY MOMENT. TIME TO MAKE IT COUNT."

The puck dropped and Cooper sprang into action, dodging
and weaving with a single goal in mind.

The shot flew past the goalie and the arena errupted with cheers. A sea of his teammates rushed over to him in excitement.

## THEY HAD WON THE STANLEY CUP!

As the ceremony followed, Cale brought the trophy over to Cooper and proudly said,

**"YOU DID IT, COOPER! YOU'RE A TRUE CHAMPION!"**

Celebrating with the team the next day during the parade, Cooper felt like he was on top of the world. His friends were all shouting,

# "YOU'RE OUR HERO, COOPER!"

Later that night, as the excitement began to calm a bit, Cooper and Velocity shared a quiet moment. "We've been through so much, Velocity. Thank you for being by my side."

Lying in bed, Cooper whispered to Velocity, "We proved that dreams can come true. Together, we can do anything."

# THE END

# ABOUT THE AUTHOR

Jack Gates is 26 years old. While playing Division 1 hockey at Colorado College, he founded Triumph Together, a nonprofit organization that helps connect collegiate and professional athletes with kids at nearby children's hospitals by getting them tickets to games, meet and greets with players, signed gear, videos of encouragement before surgery, and much more!

Jack says, "Sports are special because they give people a sense of community, hope, and most importantly something to believe in. That's what these kids need right now. They need something to look forward to, something to believe in, and to know someone is thinking of them during those extra tough days."

Triumph Together just merged with the Mitchell Thorp Foundation in order to increase their impact even more.

Find out more...
www.triumphtogether.net
(visit the above website or scan the QR code on the left)

# ABOUT COOPER

Cooper is a quick-witted, athletic 11-year-old sports enthusiast and a Colorado Avalanche fanatic. Cooper lives with a rare disease called MPS IVA, also known as Morquio Syndrome. The disease affects every organ of his body and causes severe skeletal implications including short stature. Cooper receives a four-hour infusion of medicine once per week to slow the disease progression. He's had eight surgeries so far. Although Cooper is only 38 inches tall, you will find him with his friends or big sister shooting pucks in the backyard, batting baseballs, swinging a golf club, playing video games, watching sports, or snuggling his service dog, Velocity.

Jack Gates and Triumph Together connected with Cooper and other patients at Children's Hospital Colorado during COVID. In the short time they had together playing games on a Zoom call, Jack identified Cooper as an ice hockey buff. Triumph Together has played a pivotal role in lifting Cooper's spirits since then. Cooper's favorite memory with Jack is attending the Colorado Avalanche versus Anaheim Ducks game at the Honda Center which included riding the Zamboni before the game and sharing the most delicious mini donuts from a food truck during the second period intermission.

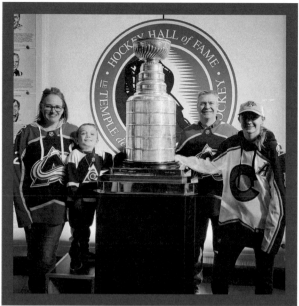

Cooper and his family visiting the Stanley Cup

Cooper and his service dog, Velocity

Cooper playing hockey in the hallway
in the hospital with his friends

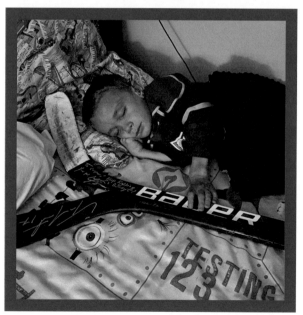

Cooper sleeping next to his sticks that were
signed by Cale Maker and Tyson Jost

# ABOUT THE ILLUSTRATOR

Daniela Frongia, also known as Caisarts, was born in 1979 in Sardinia, Italy. She is an international children's book illustrator with more than 14 years of professional experience. Since the age of 5, she was drawing Disney characters until she discovered the anime world. She graduated from art school and after various art work experiences, decided to move to London, UK, where she held her first personal art exhibition. Later, she discovered the digital world, which provided more flexibility as she loves to travel. Now, it is easier to work from anywhere with just her Wacom Cintiq.